THE BULLY EXPOSED

THE SECRETS OF DEALING WITH BULLIES AT WORK

Jonas Warstad

Published by

www.jonaswarstad.com

DISCLAIMER

The information contained in this book is for general information purposes only. In the event you use any of the information in this book for yourself, the author and the publisher assume no responsibility for your actions. The information is provided by the author, makes no representations or warranties of any kind, express or implied, about the completeness, accuracy, reliability, suitability or availability with respect to the information or related graphics contained in the book for any purpose. Any reliance you place on such information is therefore strictly at your own risk. Caveat Emptor. In no event will the author and publisher be liable for any loss or damage including without limitation, indirect or consequential loss or damage, or any loss or damage whatsoever arising from loss of data or profits arising out of, or in connection with, the use of this information provided in this book. The author takes no responsibility for, and will not be held liable for any actions from individuals arising from the information provided in this book for any reason to include acts of god and technical issues beyond our control.

Jonas Warstad has written a very important book which deals with a topic that everyone should be interested in. I find that the title, *The Bully Exposed: The Secrets of Dealing with Bullies at Work* is not only about bullies and how to deal with them, but about life and how to make it work. The author seems to have extensive knowledge and expertise in what he wrote about. He expresses his thoughts and suggestions in simple form and makes it possible for many to benefit from this work.

— 5-star Amazon review by **John Harricharan,**

Bestselling Author: *When You Can Walk on Water, Take the Boat*

***

The Bully Exposed by Jonas Warstad is a wonderful self-help resource for anyone who feels they are being "bullied" at work. Each chapter of this book is filled with great examples, insightful solutions, and suggestions on improving your own self-worth and self-confidence. A must-read for anyone who truly wants to change a seemingly negative situation into a positive experience by taking a closer look at themselves and realizing that without any victims a bully could not possibly exist!

—**Heather K. O'Hara,**

Award-winning Author: *The Path of Songs*

Table of Contents

Foreword by James Nicodemus, Attorney 6

Foreword by Mitch Darnell, Psychology Professor 8

Foreword by Traci Shoblom, M.S. Organizational Psychology 11

Prologue 15

Chapter 1 – Understanding the Bully 16

Chapter 2 – Understanding Yourself 20

Chapter 3 – Building Up Your Inner Strength 22

Chapter 4 – Dealing with the Bully 34

Chapter 5 – Six Ways to Deal with the Bully 38

Chapter 6 – Forming an Anti-Bully Group (Optional) 62

Chapter 7 – Dirty Tricks & Bluffs: Should You Use Them? 65

Epilogue 68

About Jonas Warstad 69

Connect with Jonas Warstad 71

Other Books by Jonas Warstad 72

P.S. One Last Thing... 73

Foreword by James Nicodemus, Attorney

We have heard a lot about bullies in the last 15 years. Bullies at work, bullies in school, bullies in marriage, even friends who are really bullies, we just never realized it. We are all listening now, and need to be able to sift through the hype and frenzy, and discover the good options that can truly be effective at getting bullies to stop.

As an attorney, people have asked me if you can sue a bully. Sometimes, but it would probably take years to get through the courts, and you may have to sue your employer as well, which could get technically troubling. So in the meantime, we look at other options.

This book gives a valuable summarization of dozens of ideas about bullying all distilled into a very useable how-to book. It almost reads like a logical flow chart drafted by a computer programmer. If not a, then b. If neither a nor b, than c or d.

Lawyers appreciate caselaw or facts that suggest tactical options for a plan of action. When it comes down to the crunch time in trial preparation, or witness cross-examination, you have to know your plan, map your path, and move forward with a purpose.

It is true that this book is essentially a compilation of a myriad of ideas, suggestions, medical theories and proposals that have come out of the last 15 years of discussions about bullying. Are there a lot of new ideas contained within its covers? Maybe not. But I think there is something to be said about the proposition that, after all of the town meetings, the documentaries and the self examination is done, we need a plan of action that can be digested, understood, and is presented in a way that is clear, concise, and seems accessible to real people.

This book can help real people review, understand and appreciate their options to say "No More!" to a bully starting today, and you don't need a lawyer to do it.

James Nicodemus, Attorney-at-Law, Licensed Attorney for 20 Years, Currently Practicing in State of Illinois, USA

Foreword by Mitch Darnell, Psychology Professor

Brilliantly illuminating an enduring, painful, even occasionally debilitating phenomenon, The Bully Exposed is actually for everyone regardless of their workplace experiences. Readers will find themselves depicted somewhere (and often) throughout this book. You may believe you've never been a Bully, or bullied, but you HAVE been affected by bullying whether or not you're aware of it!

"If you find yourself being bullied, you have typically been placed in one of these two categories ("strong" and "weak" people) by the bully. This can happen to the most intelligent, educated and successful people", per The Bully Exposed.. And this is absolutely, aggravatingly true!

How we end up being victimized, trapped, tricked and even humiliated by workplace Bullies is lovingly, and clearly depicted by Mr. Warstad. Sadly, an element that supports workplace bullying is lack of knowledge, awareness and appropriate, contrary beliefs and expectations.

As Mr. Warstad accurately notes, the Workplace Bully has an intense, intrinsic need to, "...show you and everyone else—by using their body language, tone of voice, and choice of words—who the social leader is and who knows best." How ironic that most who will read this book truly know that the Bully's interpretation of workplace dynamics and his/her position and outlook are far from "best". Ironically, the Workplace Bully detracts from, and even destroys, positive workplace dynamics a hundred times more than he/she contributes positively. The Victim often (definitely not always) knows that bullying is evil, mean, extremely unprofessional and unethical, and generally actually illegal.

Meanwhile, identifying what is actually transpiring when seeing and/or experiencing workplace bullying is the challenge. Readers will feel validated, and then able to understand how they may inadvertently support the bully culture and characters. Sadly, some of the best human beings unwittingly allow workplace bullying due to personality difference, contemporary workplace dynamics (such as the litigious nature of our cultures), and general confusion.

Mr. Warstad talks briefly about the "Bully's Admirers", who are actually "a part of the problem" because they actively choose to NOT "be part of the solution" via complicity and even support of the Bully's actions. How often have you chosen to walk away, look the other direction, or even maybe laugh as someone manipulates, jokes, brags, or otherwise torments one or more co-workers?

The Bully Exposed is not a legal tome providing legal advice on how to protect oneself from workplace bullies. But it IS an extremely functional, clear delineation of the dynamics, personalities and challenges involved. Readers are empowered and challenged at the same time. No one is left to their high pedestal, starting with the chapter on looking at our own "weaknesses". He even explains, without saying it, that Bullies are confused, dysfunctional human beings themselves (vs. simply being The Anti-Christ)!

Engaging cutting-edge psychotherapeutic and other healing modality techniques, The Bully Exposed introduces readers to some of the most immediately accessible, empowering methods to overcome inner and interpersonal challenges. I'm very impressed with the fact that Mr. Warstad clearly gets that there is much to be gained from practicing Eastern philosophic-based meditation and/or martial arts, along with considering Neurolinguistic Programming and Emotional Freedom Techniques. Frankly, I found reading The Bully Exposed much easier because Mr. Warstad even engages a bit of humour (i.e. when noting how many of us

9

might compare ourselves to movie martial arts characters when undertaking martial arts training), allowing us to laugh and appreciate that what he's telling you and I is that healing, empowerment and reaching our goals are all very attainable, and don't require super-human strengths!

Finally, are you ready to truly consider "The Law of Attraction"... one of the absolute, undeniable universal truths that still challenges those who wish to remain "Victims"? Throughout The Bully Exposed, the reader is treated to functional clues and ideas for dealing with workplace Bullies. He even depicts six primary psychocognitive standard impression types, and how to overcome their challenges to deal effectively with workplace Bullies.

By picking up The Bully Exposed, you've already made a positive step in the Law of Attraction. Possibly unconsciously, you're mirroring your belief that health and wellness are possible for you and/or others in your Life. The Bully Exposed is so thorough that everyone can find the sections that suit their personality and/or challenges. Trust that you are meant for this book - To be the best person YOU can be.

Mitch Darnell, MS, OSM, CRC

Psychology Professor and Psychotherapist

www.linkedin.com/in/foreverinspired

Foreword by Traci Shoblom, M.S.
Organizational Psychology

It's 6:00 am on a Monday morning and your alarm has just gone off. You hit the snooze button and roll over for ten more minutes of sleep. But, you can't fall back asleep because your mind starts dreading your day. *Ugh. We've got that staff meeting today. I can't stand Theo's smug face when he criticizes me in front of everyone. Why can't he just leave me alone? What did I ever do to him? He's always making rude comments and trying to trick me into saying something stupid. And, when they all left to go to Happy Hour on Friday and walked past my desk acting all superior—I wish I could just quit. I wonder if I could take a sick day today?*

When most people hear the term "bully," they think of the kind of harassment that takes place in school. "Anti-bullying" campaigns are commonly implemented in school systems so that innocent victims of this kind of abuse are protected.

But, what happens when bullies grow up? Do they suddenly become warm, empathetic individuals? Not likely. School bullies often grow up to become workplace bullies. They just become better at it, and more able to work within the policies and procedures of the office so that they don't get into trouble. In addition, the social norms against reporting workplace bullying are even greater. After all, you're an adult. You should be able to handle it, right? Wrong.

Workplace bullying is becoming an increasingly important problem. A recent study mentioned in *Human Resource Executive Online* reports that, "35 percent of American workers report being bullied now or at some time in their careers; 15 percent of American workers reported observing

11

bullying; 40 percent of targets *never* tell their employers about being bullied; 62 percent of bullies are men; 58 percent of targets are women; 68 percent of bullying cases involve the same gender bully and target (indeed, women account for 80 percent of bullying against other women); and 43 percent of bullying comes from co-workers (while 36 percent comes from supervisors, 12 percent from customers, 5 percent from subordinates and 4 percent from "others")
[www.hreonline.com/HRE/view/story.jhtml?id=534354451].

It's a misconception to think that bullying is simply "being rude" or "not nice." Bullying can include shouting, swearing, lying, spreading false rumors or gossip, playing mean pranks or "jokes," not including a person in relevant meetings or e-mail exchanges, excluding a person from work related social events, and other forms of intimidation.

It's also more than just a personal problem between the employees. Workplace bullying has direct costs to the business. The obvious ones are decreased productivity and higher rates of absenteeism. After all, who can work effectively when they are being harassed? But there are hidden costs as well. Being bullied in the workplace contributes to stress and anxiety, which can lead to increased medical and worker's compensation claims. Serious offenses can even lead to lawsuits in the workplace. Clearly, it's in a company's best interest to deal with workplace bullying directly.

Jonas Warstad's book *The Bully Exposed* takes a deeper look at WHY bullies behave the way they do and what victims of bullying can do to deal with the stress of being bullied in the workplace. He mentions that in order for bullying to occur, "there are five requirements: the bully, bully-friendly "admirers," someone to bully, a trigger (the bullied person does or says something that is suitable to bully) and a "clear coast" (no "anti-bully" person in authority around)." If you change one of these variables, bullying will stop.

If we are to change bullying, it's important to understand what we want to achieve in its place. It's not enough to just stop the bully. We need to address the culture in which bullying occurs. Given this, one can ask, "What is the opposite of bullying?" The opposite of bullying is empathy.

Empathy can be defined as a *shared emotional experience* occurring when one person (the subject) comes to feel *a similar emotion* to another (the object) as a result of *perceiving* the other's state. This process results from the fact that the subject's *representations* of the emotional state are *automatically* activated when the subject pays attention to the emotional state of the object [Preston, S. D. (2007). A perception-action model for empathy. In T. Farrow & P. Woodruff (Eds.), *Empathy in Mental Illness* (pp. 428–447). Cambridge: Cambridge University Press.].

In our chapter *The ACES Decision-Making Technique as a Reframing Tool for Increasing Empathy*, Dr. Larry Pate and I explain that empathy is a choice one makes in a given situation [www.routledge.com/books/details/9780415844116/].

Empathy is a function of the frame with which one is viewing the situation, self-awareness, and the ability to relate cognitively and emotionally to the other person's plight. In other words, a bully can be taught—through workplace training—how to stop bullying.

Our decision-making technique, ACES, allows a person to identify the way they are seeing a situation ("My comments don't hurt him.), reframe that situation ("My comments DO hurt him."), and to look at their mental assumptions, emotional feelings, and values about a given situation and then behave with intent.

ACES is useful in stopping the bully by teaching him or her how to reframe situations. But, what if the bully is really just a jerk who is incapable of self-awareness? ACES can also help shift the framework of the "bully-friendly admirers" by helping them feel greater empathy for the victim. Also, ACES can help the victim challenge his or her assumption that "nothing can be done." This, then, changes the culture that supports the bullying in the first place.

What's great about *The Bully Exposed* is that it helps readers to better understand that something CAN be done about workplace bullying. Jonas offers concrete suggestions on how to handle many kinds of workplace bullies. While my work is focused on helping people see things differently, Jonas takes it to the next step by teaching his readers what to do in the face of workplace bullying.

Readers of *The Bully Exposed* will develop valuable skills to help them deal with angry, controlling individuals both at work and in their personal lives. I'm honored that Jonas has asked me to write this Foreword. I think it's an important topic and I am thrilled to wholeheartedly recommend *The Bully Exposed* to readers.

"When another person makes you suffer, it is because he suffers deeply within himself, and his suffering is spilling over. He does not need punishment. He needs help."

Thich Naht Hanh

Traci Shoblom, M.S. Organizational Psychology

Management Consultant, Writer, and Senior Partner, Decision Systems International

www.ACESdecisions.com

Prologue

I don't recall ever being directly bullied until my 7th to 9th year at school, ages 13-15. That is a time when most boys get their first boost of testosterone, and some develop bully behavior. There was one boy in particular whom I remember, he selected me because he probably saw me as very "un-tough" (which I also was) and I was also the skinniest guy at school! I was also more or less a loner, meaning no one would support me. I can't say that I was bullied a lot by him though, he didn't beat me up or anything, it was more on a psychological level—but it was enough to make a lasting impression on me.

I also remember one incident around the same time at a sports camp for badminton. All kids slept there for a few nights in a large room without any supervisor, and one boy immediately spotted my "suitability" and put tooth paste all over my bag (!) while his little group of hangers-on laughed. Why he so creatively chose tooth paste, I don't know. Perhaps he is a painter today...? But nevertheless, being sensitive these incidents stuck with me and I started thinking about why people would act like that. I was always a deep thinker...

After those three years I was never really bullied, but I kept studying people. And this book is one of the results of my "study of human and un-human behavior".

Jonas Warstad

Chapter 1 – Understanding the Bully

1. What characterizes a "work bully"?

While many things change when we finally leave school and get a job, some things never change: there will still be bullies. Although "work bullies" can be more "subtle" in their methods and usually won't bully you physically, they behave more or less the same way that school-bullies behave: they make fun of you by pointing out "peculiarities" in your looks (loud and clear for everyone to hear), they call you names and make ironic or sarcastic remarks about you, they say bad things about you behind your back, etc.

2. Why is the bully acting like this?

A bully is unable to relate to people in an "equal" way—they *must* be at the "social top". It's their ulterior motive, wired deeply into their brains. They know of no other way of living than to be recognized by everyone as the "top social leader". At the same time they also typically feel a need to *prove* their top status to their (real or imagined) "admirers" by bullying people in order to demonstrate or restore the social rank/pecking order (where they are naturally at the top).

3. What do they gain from it?

The bully's reward is the reactions they get from their "admirers" in the form of admiration, awe, laughter, etc., which the bully interprets as "we approve of and respect you as our leader" (if the bully feels that they are at the center of everyone's attention and admiration they can even be charming!). There are also bullies with a strain of sadism who revel even without an admiring audience, in which case their reward is the good feeling they get from making someone feel bad. In either case, the way to deal with them is basically the same, but the "evil/sadistic" bully usually requires the "toughest" solutions.

4. Who is the bully?

Bullying is typically performed by the "social leader" (this does not mean that all social leaders are bullies, but all bullies are or aim to be social leaders). At workplaces it is the executive/boss who is the "formal leader", but that does not automatically make them the social leader, especially not in larger groups where the boss cannot be present at all times and oversee everything personally. Sometimes the bullying is performed by the social leader's immediate "social subordinates" on direct or implied order from the leader.

It's actually quite easy to "test" if someone (not an actual executive) considers themselves the social leader of their group: simply question something they said or did, in front of everyone (if you want to be really provocative you can say, "No, no, you are wrong!"). If they are the social leader, they will usually get very defensive and show you and everyone else—by using their body language, tone of voice and choice of words—who the social leader is and who knows best. If they are not the leader, they will often refer to the leader in their reply, nodding their head in the leader's direction. It could also happen that it *is* the leader, but one of their "social subordinates" steps in immediately like a guard in their defense. Whatever happens, it will give you valuable clues.

5. Who are the bully's "admirers"?

Anyone who seeks acceptance from the bully. Why do they do that? Because they want to feel like "one of the gang" (even if in reality they are only a sheep in the flock, ruled and pushed around by a wolf). And why do they want to be in the gang when it's ruled by someone who obviously does not respect them? Because they have low self-confidence and would rather project or "externalize" their confidence onto someone else whom they consider "strong" to act confidently in their place.

6. Who does the bully attack, and why?

In order for a bully to remain at the top of the social rank at a workplace (as they view it) they have a habit of attacking both "strong" and "weak" people. If you find yourself being bullied, you have typically been placed in one of these two categories by the bully. This can happen to the most intelligent, educated and successful people.

Strong people are potential "threats to the throne" and need to be "put in place" every now and then—just in case! It could be that what someone said, or the way they said it, signaled "disrespect" to them. It could be that someone did not greet them the right way and they were offended. It could be that they feel challenged or threatened by someone's (real or imagined) opinions, political views, attitude, gender, status, money, power, etc. Only the bullies themselves know the real reason, and sometimes they are not even aware of why they feel the way they do—it may be a subconscious reaction triggered in some hidden parts deep inside their brain.

The reason why they also try to push "weak" people down is because the bully can *appear* stronger by increasing the *distance* between themselves and the person they bully by lowering their already low status. How does the bully know someone is weak? By observing their reactions: if someone reacts by getting sad or afraid (and especially if that makes onlookers laugh) they know they're weak! It could also be the way someone looks or walks or uses their body language that annoys them or signals "weakness". Another common sign is when the bully notices that someone does not understand that they are being made fun of and looks totally perplexed when "everybody" laughs. Bullies are experts at observing and noticing other people's "weaknesses". In this sense bullies are like animal predators that prefer to attack weakened or injured prey—and thus in a way also like human predators: psychopaths.

Chapter 2 – Understanding Yourself

Why do the bully's words hurt?

A bully's words and/or actions will typically hurt under three conditions: 1) if you are sensitive about something particular in your persona or looks, 2) if you have low self-confidence/self-value in general, or 3) if your subconscious mind connects what the bully said with something someone else said to you long ago (or any combination of these three).

Bullies take advantage of all of these psychological "buttons" and fire them off in people's minds, knowing full well that it will make some feel annoyed, nervous, intimidated, embarrassed, ashamed, humiliated, inferior or worthless (or even suicidal, even though it's not certain that a bully knowingly wants to go that far—worthless is usually far enough to them, but bullies are not known to think very far).

Why then do some people feel bad or worthless because of a bully's words, while others are not affected so deeply, even if it's the same bully and the same words? The difference, naturally, lies in the bullied person. People who feel confident about themselves and who truly believe they are worth just as much as everybody else will usually not feel worthless because of a bully's words, but will either get angry and tell the bully off, or just not care because they don't feel any reaction from what the bully says about them (because in their mind it just isn't true).

An excellent demonstration, albeit exaggerated to make a comedy out of it, is the 1987 comedy movie *Roxanne* where Steve Martin plays a man who, in spite of a nose so oversized that only his mother could love it, has tremendous self-confidence and thus deep inside does not agree even a bit with anyone who claims his nose is "ugly".

On the contrary, he challenges any bully and hammers them down with ease psychologically and intellectually, as well as physically.

Chapter 3 – Building Up Your Inner Strength

If you, for some reason, have absolutely no aspirations whatsoever to become stronger as a person, or if you were "born tough" and feel absolutely no need to build up your inner strength and you just want to get on with the "real deal" as soon as possible, you may skip this chapter and go directly to *Chapter 4 – Dealing with the Bully.* I recommend though that you at least *read through* this chapter and only then decide if you want to skip it or not.

If you, on the other hand, want to take the time to build up your inner strength (and possibly even aiming at being able to take on the bully yourself) then read on—there are more than enough "mental tricks" here in Chapter 3 to help you. By building up your inner strength you will become less susceptible to the bully's words, and thus stronger and better prepared to confront them.

(For more information and links to any of the methods I mention below, please see www.jonaswarstad.com)

1. Working on Your Weakness

In order to work on your weakness, you first need to determine whether you are sensitive about something *particular* in your persona or looks, if you have low self-confidence/self-value *in general*, or if the problem lies in your *subconscious.*

If you know that you are **sensitive about something particular** in your persona or looks, and/or you have noticed that the bully is successfully using the same "button" every time, it means that deep inside you agree with the bully, have accepted them as authority, and place value in their "opinion". In short: the words hurt because the bully "acknowledges" what you already "know". Thus, in order to work on your weakness, you need to address the way you view yourself and the bully. Remember, this is the difference between a bullied person and a person who is not affected.

There are different ways to address "weak spots" in yourself. Perhaps the most obvious way is with the help of a psychologist, using various "desensitization" techniques. If you feel this is right for you, and you can afford it, I suggest seeing a psychologist.

Another option is hypnosis. Somewhat surrounded by misconceptions and mystique, hypnosis, if performed by a licensed professional, is in fact an excellent and efficient way to deal with "weak spots", as it addresses the subconscious mind directly. You can also use self-hypnosis MP3s or CDs which have the advantage of being far cheaper than seeing a hypnotist, and you can listen to them in the comfort of your own home. I recommend a self-hypnosis recording aimed at general self-confidence.

There are also "alternative" methods, like "EFT" (Emotional Freedom Techniques), which in a sense is related to classic acupuncture, but instead of needles you tap gently with your finger tips on specific meridian points on your head, face, etc., while focusing on the thing that bothers you—in this case your reactions when the bully tries to bully you. If done properly, the negative feelings/emotions will often diminish or even vanish completely. If you ask people who have used it, EFT is usually considered a very efficient, versatile and gentle method that is also relatively easy to learn to use on yourself.

If you have **low self-confidence** and/or the bully is successful no matter what they do or say, then your problem typically lies in the way you view yourself and your self-worth; you simply don't think you are worth as much as everybody else. If you don't feel worthy of being treated with respect, your low self-confidence and self-worth will attract the bully like a moth to the flame. Thus, in order to work on your confidence, you need to address the way you view yourself. Remember, this is the difference between a bullied person and a person who is not affected.

The way to address low confidence is more or less the same as when you are sensitive about something particular (see above), but seeing a psychologist about "low confidence" may take a long time and be quite costly. Here, perhaps hypnosis or self-hypnosis is a better/faster alternative for you. (For self-hypnosis I recommend a recording aimed at general self-confidence or a specialized recording called "No More Mr. Nice Guy" or "No More Ms. Doormat." I also recommend EFT, the versatile method which can also work wonderfully on low confidence.

Besides working on building up your confidence from within, I recommend that you also start building up your self-confidence "from the outside in", starting with walking and talking *as if you were* self-confident already ("fake it until you make it"!). If you feel unworthy and not confident, it most certainly shows—so take a good and honest look at yourself in a mirror. Bad body posture (your own subconscious way of making you appear shorter, to match your low self-worth) and head bent forward (to avoid eye contact) are typical signs of low confidence, and bullies are often experts at noticing that! The theory behind this is that if you walk, stand and talk confidently, your brain will produce "strength" hormones—you will *feel* different. Thus you will start a positive chain of events where you *feel* better and more confident, which leads to *acting* more confident, which in turn makes you feel even more confident, etc. Practice this at home. Study confident people on TV or in films; observe how they walk and talk, and try to copy them. But don't overdo it: find a style that looks natural to you. (This is a technique inspired by NLP, Neuro-Linguistic Programming.)

If you are **not sure** why you react so strongly, it probably means that the problem lies hidden in your subconscious. If your subconscious mind connects what the bully says with something that someone else said to you long ago, even in your childhood, the bully's words could trigger an old similar event in your subconscious, and now this brings out the same feeling of worthlessness that you had way back then (time does not exist in your subconscious mind, but it remembers absolutely everything!).

Read through the various methods for when you are sensitive about something in particular and for low confidence (see above), and notice if some method(s) seem to be the right thing for you. Besides taking your budget into consideration, also listen to your intuition, what your gut feeling tells you. If you don't feel like any of these methods are for you, don't worry, just read on and you will be guided through further steps to make you prepared to confront the bully.

2. Building Inner Strength

Aside from the obvious support you can get from friends and family, there are other ways of increasing your inner strength, if you feel you want or need that. If you are religious, you can get inner strength through the support from your local church and by praying to God or any Higher Force you believe in. Hope and comfort and a belief in a Higher Justice will give you strength.

If "Eastern" philosophies appeal to you, you may also find inner strength in meditation, yoga, Tai Chi or Qigong. These forms of exercises have been used for thousands of years in many countries to gain inner strength and balance. Meditation is the most "still" form, while the others involve movements and breathing techniques to a lesser or larger degree. Learning directly from a qualified teacher is the best. If you can't find a teacher near you or are unsure which practice suits you best, I recommend books and DVDs to give you an idea of what it is about. Remember to always check with your physician before starting any practice.

Another practice that may appeal to you is self defense/martial arts, which may give you a deeper sense of confidence than mere meditation and yoga can give you, because the martial arts also focus on self-discipline, self-respect and learning to honor and maintain your own personal boundaries against physical intrusions. There are literally hundreds of forms of martial arts originating from all corners of the planet. I suggest you pick a form that is relatively easy to learn, like karate, because the truth is that most forms of martial arts are relatively complicated and it can take a lot of time to learn or master them. The risk here is, if your heroes are Bruce Lee, Steven Seagal, Jet Li or Jean-Claude Van Damme and you compare yourself to them but fail to live up to your own expectations, then your "failure" may be the thing that sinks your already low confidence into rock bottom. You need to be realistic and use heroes as inspiration, not goals. Remember that they have not only trained for many, many years, but they are also huge natural talents with an incredible determination. I am not saying *you* cannot do it, all I am saying is, don't let your confidence stand or fall with you becoming a black belt. Karate is one of the best known forms of martial arts, and one reason for this is of course the 1984 youth movie *Karate Kid.* While it is, of course, full of romanticized Hollywood ideas about how fast one can learn karate and how to deal with an attacker or bully, it does have a point about what martial arts can do for a person's self-confidence. If you feel that it would better help your confidence and inner strength if you were able to defend yourself in "real street" scenarios as simply and efficiently as possible without any "fancy" complicated moves, I suggest you learn the military based Krav Maga or some other form of close quarters combat from a personal trainer (or possibly from a good DVD). As always, check with your physician before starting any practice.

3. Mental Preparation before Confronting the Bully – Part 1: NLP

By now, if you have done all the preparatory steps, you should be much better prepared to confront the bully. But there is yet another way to prepare yourself: through NLP (Neuro-Linguistic Programming), a term we touched upon briefly in the previous part "Working on Your Weakness" where you study confident people and walk and talk like they do.

The associations you have in your subconscious mind about someone decide what your mind "sees" (an annoying person? a person to be afraid of? a neutral person?) and thus dictate how you will feel and react when you meet them—or even when you think about them. An NLP "secret" is that you can actually consciously change those associations using NLP techniques, and thus decrease or totally remove your negative reactions. (Much like using "EFT" in the previous part "Working on Your Weakness," but instead of working on your body's "energy system" you work on the psychological associations in your subconscious.)

There are three aspects to this that you can address with NLP: how your subconscious mind views whom the bully is attacking, how it views onlookers and, finally, how it views the relationship between you and the bully.

In order to address **how your subconscious views whom the bully is attacking**, bring to mind someone you love dearly and feel very protective about—it could be your spouse, your child, a younger sibling, or even a pet. It can even be an object like your car or some object which has an "affection value" to you—whatever brings out the protective instincts in you! Then imagine ("visualize") that the bully is attacking not only you, but also the person you love (who is standing next to you).

Normally this will automatically bring out "blind anger" in you, meaning anger unaffected by any sort of fear—the kind of anger a lioness would feel toward any attacker that threatens her offspring, even if that attacker is much larger. This shift of emotion will take place virtually instantly, because "fear" hormones (adrenaline, etc.) and "anger" hormones are basically identical. The idea here is to change your subconscious from associating the bully's target with "me" to "someone I love".

A funny example is when Ms. Parker confronts Mr. Raines in the episode *"Keys"* in Season 1 of the excellent TV series *"The Pretender"* (which ran from 1996-2001). Ms. Parker had been profoundly afraid of Mr. Raines for some time; not only because he was her superior, but because of his looks (Nosferatu) and his intimidating ways in general, including breathing through an oxygen tank. But when she suddenly remembered a frightening scene from when she was a child and saw a repressed memory of her mother being beaten up by Mr. Raines (at least that's what she concluded), everything changed, because now her subconscious no longer associated Mr. Raines with "someone I am terribly afraid of" but with "someone who beat up my mother". This slight change in perspective had the effect of turning her fear into cold, pure anger. I believe that the resulting confrontation is a perfect illustration of her new perspective. A later, even more impressive confrontation, is in the episode *"Over the Edge"* in Season 2 when she totally shows him who he is dealing with. (Craig W. Van Sickle and Steven Long Mitchell, the creators of The Pretender, are now continuing the Pretender saga at www.thepretenderlives.com)

In order to address **how your subconscious views onlookers**, bring to mind "silly" people or characters, real or fictitious, the opinions and views of someone you could not care less about. It could be ridiculous looking little gnomes, or the Smurfs ®, or whatever characters you have seen in films or read about in comic books that represent "silly characters" to you. Or, why not the laughing rat-like little creature that is Jabba the Hutt's pet in the 1983 Star Wars movie, *"Return of the Jedi"*—and whose ridiculous appearance and unforgettable laughter is shown at 9:50, 10:26, 20:40 and, perhaps best, 21:17 into the movie (the timings are based on the DVD in the 2011 Blu-ray Star Wars Box *"The Complete Saga"*).

Then bring to mind the bully's onlookers, or how they usually look to you. See both the onlookers and the "silly" character(s) in front of you, with your inner eye ("visualize"). Notice where the onlookers are located compared to where the "silly" characters are located. Most likely they are far from each other; this is your subconscious mind's way of separating things that "don't go together".

Now, gradually and consciously move the bully's onlookers toward the "silly" characters, while you also change the onlooker's attributes to look like the "silly" characters' attributes. An example: if you choose "Smurfs ®" then, as Step 1, make the onlookers tiny and blue, and move them a step towards the Smurfs ®. In Step 2 you change the onlooker's appearance further, like the body shape, and give them silly, high-pitched voices, and move them even further toward the Smurfs ®. Do this in as many steps as feels natural to you, until the onlookers have merged completely with the Smurfs ®.

Do this mental exercise several times per day for at least three weeks, until you feel the scene has been "etched" into your subconscious and feels automatic and natural, and brings a nice, confident smile to your face. The idea here is to stop your subconscious from associating the onlookers with "people I dread to appear stupid in front of" and, instead, making it associate them with "silly characters whose opinions I could not care less about". Remember that the subconscious mind is incredibly strong compared to your conscious mind (power of will and logical reasoning) and until you control the subconscious, it will control you.

Finally, in order to address **how your subconscious views the relationship between you and the bully**, bring to mind someone you are not afraid of. It may be someone you usually laugh at, perhaps a comedy actor or a clown or a cartoon figure, or perhaps someone you know who you definitely are not afraid of, like a younger sibling or a friend. Then bring to mind your bully. See them both in front of you, with your inner eye ("visualize"). Notice where the bully is located compared to where the person you are not afraid of is located. Most likely they are far from each other, because this is your subconscious mind's way of separating things that "don't go together".

Now, gradually and consciously move the bully toward the person you are not afraid of while you also change the bully's attributes to look like the other person's attributes. An example: if you choose "Mickey Mouse ®" then, as Step 1, give the bully big, black, round ears and a small, black nose, and move him a step toward Mickey. In Step 2 you change the bully's appearance further, like the face and hands and a silly high-pitched voice, and move him even further towards Mickey. Do this in as many steps as feels natural to you, until the bully has merged with Mickey and has become him. (If you had chosen a clown, you would have put a clown nose and large, silly shoes on your bully, etc.)

Do this mental exercise several times per day for at least three weeks, until you feel the scene has been "etched" into your subconscious and feels automatic and natural, and brings a nice, confident smile to your face. The idea here is stop your subconscious from associating the bully with "someone I am afraid of" and, instead, making it associate them with "someone I am *not* afraid of".

Next, bring to mind someone you associate with the kind of confidence that you would like to have. Only you know what person, real or imagined, is your ideal or role model; it may be a martial arts master or super hero or actor, or it may be a "real life" confident person.

Imagine in your mind ("visualize") how they would deal with the person who bullies you; how they would stand firm and tall, put their palm a foot from the bully's chest (like a policeman would to stop a person) and with a stern facial expression, fearlessly telling the bully to "Back off!" (This is only an example; you can use any variation that feels right for you.) Involve as many senses as possible: see the person in front of you, hear them talk to the bully, feel the confidence that radiates from them, etc.

Do this mental exercise several times per day for at least three weeks, until you feel the scene has been "etched" into your subconscious and feels automatic and natural and brings a nice, confident smile to your face. The idea here is stop your subconscious from associating the bully with "someone who *cannot* be dealt with" and, instead, making it associate the bully with "someone who *can* be dealt with".

Now it's time for the "grand finale" by tying together all your mental visualizations into a "play" where you actually move around physically and speak out loud. Make sure you can do this alone in peace and quiet—this is quite a delicate step psychologically, and if someone sees you and laughs at you at this point, even if it's just your spouse, it may undermine your confidence or even ruin the process.

Start by slowly but steadily taking the place of your "hero". Step into your hero and imagine that you become them. Imagine yourself standing firm and tall, putting your palm a foot from the bully's chest (like a policeman would to stop a person) and with a stern facial expression, fearlessly telling the bully to "Back off!" (This is only an example. You can use any variation that feels right for you.) Involve as many senses as possible when you watch yourself: talk to the bully, feel the confidence that radiates from you, etc.

Gradually involve the previous "visualizations" into the scene: change any onlookers into "silly characters", imagine that the person you love and feel very protective about is standing next to you and is also being attacked by the bully, and change the bully's appearance into whatever "silly" appearance you have chosen.

Do this exercise daily for at least three weeks, until you feel that your image of yourself as a "hero" has been "etched" into your subconscious and feels automatic and natural, and brings a nice, confident smile to your face. The final goal here is to stop your subconscious from associating the bully with "someone a really confident person can deal with" and, instead, making it associate them with "someone *I* can deal with".

4. Mental Preparation before Confronting the Bully – Part 2: Law of Attraction

The Law of Attraction, or LOA for short, basically states that what you think about and focus on, you also get more of—regardless of whether it's something "positive" or something "negative." It also states that LOA is in action at all times, whether you are aware of this Law or not—as is every other natural law, like the law of gravity. This means, according to LOA, that the more your thoughts (and thus your feelings) revolve around the bully, the more you will "attract" the bully. (If you use NLP to visualize the bully in an altered appearance you are actually using LOA, unknowingly, to attract the bully, but in a "handleable" form.)

LOA is probably best known from the 2006 film and book *The Secret,* but there were actually several books published around 100 years before that on that topic! (Amongst them a book called *Thought Vibration - the Law of Attraction in the Thought World.*) While the true origins of LOA are hidden behind centuries and possibly millennia of mysticism, variations of LOA appear in the Bible ("as you sow so shall you reap") as well as in the Eastern philosophies as "karma". However, instead of the common idea in the world's largest religions that "what you *do* shall return your way," LOA is focusing on your *thoughts:* "What you *think and feel* shall return your way".

If you feel that LOA is something that you want to try, the basic principle is extremely easy to learn: focus in your mind and emotions on what you *want*—not what you *don't* want. But just as easy as it is to learn, just as difficult it can be for some to actually follow it! In the case of a bully, LOA states that the more you think about and focus on the bully, the more you will attract the bully into your life. In order to complement all the previous mental processes, you can apply LOA in this way: unless you are using NLP to visualize the bully—do not think about the bully! Think about people you like and love, people who are nice to you and who support you; in short, the people you *want* in your life. You can also use LOA to visualize (using as many senses as possible) how you successfully deal with the bully.

Chapter 4 – Dealing with the Bully

1. Why is the bully attacking you?

Based on the information in *Chapter 1 – Understanding the Bully*, take a look at yourself through the eyes of the bully. What do you see? Why do they target you? (I am not saying it's your own fault—I am saying that you can become stronger through self-awareness and knowledge.) Questions that can help you are: Is there any common denominator in their attacks, or are they attacking seemingly random targets in you? Are you the only one around who is being bullied, or are there more? If there are more, is there a common denominator?

Ask people you trust, especially close friends and family, because they know you better and will probably be totally honest with you, why they think that *you* are being targeted by the bully. Then think carefully about this, draw your own conclusions, and write down what *about you* the bully is attacking.

2. Should you change something about yourself?

You can typically place any of your "weak targets" (as the bully sees it) in one of four categories: 1) Something you *can* do something about and also *want* to change, like "weak" behavior, etc. 2) Something you *can* do something about but *don't want* to change (opinions, hair style, etc.) 3) Something you generally *can't* do anything about but *want* to change (stuttering, shortness of height, etc.) 4) Something you generally *can't* do anything about and also *don't want* to change (perhaps some hereditary physical or personal traits).

By being aware of what it is *about you* that the bully is targeting, you can decide whether you want to (or can) change your "weakness" or not. Only you can decide that it is within your power to either change, in order to try to avoid the bully's attacks, or not to change (for whatever reason).

Some funny examples of awareness and whether to change or not in connection with bullying are two scenes from the by now classic 2004 "nerd comedy" *Napoleon Dynamite*. In the first scene, starting at 6:13, Napoleon (excellently portrayed by Jon Heder) brags about how he and his uncle "spent all last summer in Alaska hunting wolverines and shot fifty of them using a 12-gauge gun". In the second scene, starting at 15:44, Napoleon is "singing" using deaf sign language to soft music together with five girls in front of the whole class.

In the first scene, naturally the bullies know he's lying; but the reason why they make fun of him is probably not so much because he is lying, but rather because he thinks they actually believe him! If Napoleon had been aware of all that (or if he cared in the first place–we never know with Napoleon) and had chosen to stop lying, they would probably not bully him (at least not for that reason!). But then again lying and bragging probably are the things that make him feel important in the first place, and if he stopped that, then perhaps he would lose that feeling of being important. So, these decisions are not always clear-cut to the bullied person. In the second scene—although we will never know whether he is aware that the bully is watching, scornfully shaking his head—*if* Napoleon *was* aware that he was being watched, he would also have a choice whether to stop doing "girlish" things in public or not.

3. When will the bully attack?

In order for an attack to occur, there are five requirements: the bully, bully-friendly "admirers", someone to bully, a trigger (the bullied person does or says something that is suitable to bully) and a "clear coast" (no "anti-bully" person in authority around). If any part is missing, there will probably be no attack. The exception is when the bully gets satisfaction from bulling you without any onlookers.

4. How can you predict an attack?

The bully and their closest admirers are usually very "tight" and keep constant eye-contact just in case a "suitable victim" to bully comes up. Mutual eye contact and a smirk on their faces signals full awareness and agreement, and a nod in the direction of the target from the bully is usually all it takes to start the bullying.

By carefully observing them and what signals they use to communicate, you will be able to predict attacks (and thus to some degree also prevent them). If you feel you need to improve your skills in reading faces, I suggest you study books on general face reading. Or why not combine business with pleasure by watching the TV series "Lie To Me"? Even if it's fiction, it focuses heavily on the theory of facial expressions and general body language.

5. What will make the bully stop?

A bully will continue to bully until someone they perceive as equally powerful or more powerful makes them stop. That person can be either your mutual boss, a co-worker of yours whom they feel respect for, a representative of the law enforcement (e.g. a judge), or you yourself.

I like to use the symbols of wolf, sheep flock, lone-sheep, lone-wolf and Guardian Dog here. The bully is a wolf; the people who admire or follow the bully are the sheep flock; the person they bully (or rather who allows himself to be bullied) is a lone-sheep; anyone who opposes the wolf and stands up for themselves is a lone-wolf (meaning a "good" wolf who is not interested in bullying others); and anyone who stands up for themselves as well as for others, either by nature or through their occupation, is a Guardian Dog.

6. How well "protected" are you from being bullied at work?

State laws and the way the laws are applied are different in different countries when it comes to "bullying" (psycho-social workplace laws, verbal violations, etc.). In some countries it's illegal and the law is forcefully implemented; in some countries it's illegal but only in theory, and in practice no one cares; in other countries it's not illegal and everyone is on their own. Find out what *your* state laws say about bullying.

When it comes to individual companies, some more caring companies, regardless of state laws, have strict "anti-bully" rules (codes of behavior), while other companies could care less and reason that there are plenty of unemployed people out there, and if any employee feels bullied then they can just quit and look for jobs elsewhere. Find out what *your* company's rules are.

Even if there are no specified laws for codes of behavior, keep in mind that an organization, after all, consists of individuals, and chances are that your boss (or your boss's boss) actually cares as a human being, or knows that you're a valuable asset and will protect you regardless of any flaws in the state laws or company policy. And even if your boss is weak, there is still a chance that a "Guardian Dog" co-worker could come to your rescue.

Chapter 5 – Six Ways to Deal with the Bully

Option 1: If you for various reasons won't or can't deal with the bully yourself (for example if you feel intimidated by them) and you feel that your workplace/country has decent behavior codex/laws and/or that your boss is able and willing to support you, your best option is to deal with the bully via an authority. Go to <u>Option 1</u>.

Option 2: If you won't or can't deal with the bully yourself, and your boss or company are not able or willing to support you, or if you don't want to be seen as "weak" by asking your boss for help or take legal measures, your best option is to deal with the bully with the help of a strong ally. Go to <u>Option 2</u>.

Option 3: If you won't or can't deal with the bully yourself and you can't find a strong ally, your best option is to deal with the bully with support and comfort from other bullied co-workers. Go to <u>Option 3</u>.

Option 4: If you need to deal with the bully alone and you are a "soft" non-confrontational personality and want to avoid direct involvement with the bully as much as possible, your best option is to write the bully a "smart" letter. Go to <u>Option 4</u>.

Option 5: If you want to or need to deal with the bully alone and you are a "soft" non-confrontational personality, but want to learn how to take on the bully yourself eye-to-eye, this is the option for you. Go to <u>Option 5</u>.

Option 6: If you are the "tough" confrontational personality and prefer to deal with the bully yourself, your best option is to confront the bully in a "smart" way that doesn't challenge them unnecessarily. Go to <u>Option 6</u>.

Option 1: Dealing With The Bully Via An Authority

If you are the softer, non-confrontational personality and for various reasons won't or can't deal with the bully yourself (for example if you feel intimidated by them) and you feel that your workplace/country has decent behavior codex/laws and/or that your boss is able and willing to support you, you just need to inform your boss and hope they will believe in you and work actively against the bully. The only drawback is that you risk being seen as "weak" by the bully and their members, but if you can live with that, it's probably a price you are willing to pay.

If you want it to be solved properly, you will need to be persistent and keep up a tough attitude towards your boss/company. If you take half-measures, like only asking your boss once and if it doesn't work out, you stop pushing your boss because you don't want to be "pushy", then it will not work.

Even if your boss doesn't directly disbelieve you (it's likely that they are aware of their subordinate's bullying tendencies) they will probably want something tangible to go by when confronting the bully with your accusations, so do your homework and write down things they say or do to you, with date and time. Do this every time it happens, for at least a week, or as long as you feel is necessary to show that it's a pattern, not just a couple of isolated incidents.

It's also a good idea to write down the names of anyone who was there and witnessed it; in this way your boss can verify your story with them. But ask your boss to approach them discretely since people tend to be afraid of the bully and would probably not be willing to "testify" unless they feel they can do so safely and anonymously.

If you feel it's necessary to convince your boss, and it's legal in your country and/or at your workplace, use a hidden recorder and record it all; wear it at all times, and be ready to press the record button discretely as soon as the bully approaches you. Just make sure you don't "provoke" them to say things to you, as that may be used against you—just act naturally, and let the bully do the same!

As long as your boss is doing his job as a boss, and your company has a strict policy against bullying, there is no reason why this should not solve the situation for you. Being a "social leader" does not count for much at a workplace where the "formal leader" (your mutual boss) has the real authority and power to correct situations or people who obstruct work. Remember, though, that it cannot stop the bullying person's attitude, thoughts or opinions—only what they say and do to you—but if you can live with that, that too is probably a price you are willing to pay.

Should it turn out that your boss is unable to deal with it in a satisfactory way (because they are afraid of the bully or think you are not important enough), bring up the case with their boss (and so on). Should that still not solve it, it means your company policy isn't working as it should in practice. If there is a legal and working trade union, let them do the negotiations with your boss(es) for you.

If not, you have two choices. Either move on to Option 2, or inform the highest executive that if they don't resolve it, you will be forced to take legal measures. It's likely that they will want to avoid the negative publicity, and thus increase their efforts. Remember, you are not threatening them in any illegal way; you are giving them an honest last chance to fix the situation.

Option 2: Dealing With The Bully With The Help Of A Strong Ally

If you are the softer, non-confrontational personality and for various reasons won't or can't deal with the bully yourself, and feel that your workplace/country has non-existent or non-functional behavior codex/laws, and/or that your boss/trade union is not able or willing to support you, or if you don't want to be seen as "weak" by asking your boss/trade union for help or take legal measures, then your best option is to deal with the bully with the help of a strong ally—a strong co-worker with whom you have a common "enemy" (the bully). There are two kinds of strong co-workers: "lone-wolves" and "Guardian Dogs".

Their combination of being independent and their low tolerance level for people in general means that lone-wolves simply don't "like people" that much and thus don't really care what people think about them—which makes them a hard target for bullies. Not only will they *not* cringe if people laugh at them because of what a bully says about them; they will also *not* be afraid of the bully, because that fear is often based on fear of loss of social status, a game that lone-wolves simply don't play. And, as a result, they won't hesitate for a second to give the bully a severe telling-off, in front of everyone, should they ever try anything with them.

Guardian Dogs have the same inner strength as lone-wolves, but their field of responsibility naturally stretches outside of their own sphere. Their "Robin Hood" attitude to social justice means that they take responsibility for everyone, and they especially protect the weak. They will forcefully hammer down on anyone they feel is saying or doing something unfair to someone else—exactly the opposite of a wolf! Because of this, a Guardian Dog is the wolf's natural arch enemy, and wolves hate them even more than they hate lone-wolves.

In an ideal world, every workplace has at least one Guardian Dog (who preferably has also been granted some formal power). If your workplace has one, congratulations! As long as it's a relatively small workplace, they will naturally sniff out any bully and handle them then and there, using their natural fearlessness and authority. When a Guardian Dog shines light on a wolf's shady intentions, any onlookers will typically feel ashamed and at the same time be impressed by the strength and purity of the Guardian Dog's intentions, and reject the wolf because he will seem weak.

Typical signs that a workplace has a Guardian Dog is a relaxed social atmosphere, smiling workers, and an absence of obvious bullies. If someone tries "wolf manners", perhaps a newcomer, people will just smile and say, "Oh [X] will deal with him soon". (For that same reason some people will even enjoy wolves, because they can't wait to see them being "shot down" by the Guardian Dog!) Even if your workplace is large, a Guardian Dog will be well known and it will not take much detective work to find them, now that you know what to look for. Any trade union would surely also know about them.

However, in the real world not all workplaces have a Guardian Dog, and while a boss would seem to be a natural Guardian Dog, it's not at all certain that they are one by nature (even if it is, or should be, their job to act like one). They may in fact even be a sheep as a person and deep inside fear the bully themselves, thus giving the bully free reins. In these cases they are both more or less consciously aware of that, and have a silent mutual agreement "You leave me alone and I leave you alone". So never assume your boss is or will act like a Guardian Dog.

If there is no Guardian Dog, your second best chance is to find a lone-wolf. So how do you find one? By knowing the typical signs of a lone-wolf, by observing people, and by observing the bully.

Typical signs of a lone-wolf are: more or less unsocial by nature (hence their name!), so they are much more likely to be found keeping to themselves than socializing with others or in a group. Often, but not always, lone-wolves are "old-timers" —people who have worked there for a long time and have seen many people come and go.

Observe people: Because a lone-wolf is neither afraid of nor admires the bully, you can rule out anyone who laughs with the bully or reacts in any condoning way when the bully bullies you or anyone else (because they fear or admire the bully), and you can rule out anyone who lets the bully bully them (because they fear the bully).

Observe the bully: Even if a bully wants everyone to be in their sheep flock, they will not waste their time on anyone who is obviously not a sheep. Met with too much resistance, a bully will simply avoid certain people and leave them alone and focus their time and energy on the "easy hangers-on". It's these "left-alone" people who are your potential allies. So look for any co-worker of yours who the bully seems to avoid.

A bully will typically not look in the direction of someone they avoid, fear or have respect for (not counting "natural" exceptions like their boss), and that person will also typically not look at the bully. At most they will both exchange a very brief, almost undetectable mutual eye contact without turning their heads or greet in any way, as if saying "I know you exist, but this place is really not big enough for the both of us". They will simply pretend the other person does not exist, and only talk when and if their job duties force them to do so; only saying what is necessary—in a short and impersonal way—and usually avoiding any eye contact.

Make notes, until you think you have found every lone-wolf. Now it's time for you to decide who on your list you should approach first. If you did not find anyone, go to Option 3 below. If there is only one person on the list, make a decision to approach them, as they are your best hope at this point. If it's more than one person, pick the one who seems the most "open" and friendly, because they are usually also the most helpful and caring (as caring as lone-wolves can be).

A good time to approach them is when they are not involved in any conversation (obviously) and when you are both out of hearing distance from others. It does not matter if the bully or others see you together.... let them wonder! If applicable, present yourself courteously and briefly, then say, "I would like to ask you for some advice in confidence, is that OK?" In all likelihood they will say "yes" because the fact that someone acknowledges their point of view and experience usually makes them feel valuable. You could say, "I have noticed that [The Bully] doesn't seem to like me, and because [The Bully] does not seem to bother you, I figured that you might have some advice for me".

In response they may give you advice like, "Oh, he does that with all newcomers, just ignore him", or "He just dislikes people who give him advice in front of others". They may also give you information on any weak spot the bully might have or suggest some other way to deal with the bully, such as: "Just do like I do, tell him to #¤%&" [Censored!] Remember that a lone-wolf does not necessarily know of or use "weak spots". They may not know of any "smart" way to "avoid" the bully—they often simply tell the bully off, because they have a natural inner strength that bullied people often lack.

Ask as many lone-wolves and old-timers as you can and draw your own conclusions about why the bully bullies you and not them. Should you now feel inspired to become or act like a "lone-wolf" yourself and deal with the bully on your own, go to Option 4. If not, your best option now is to try and befriend your new contacts, the lone-wolves. The bullies have a natural respect for them, and if you can make the bully mentally associate you with "the other wolves" it is possible that the bully will leave you alone. There are two ways to go about it: either ask the lone-wolf right away to help you actively with the bully, or slowly build up a relationship and hope they will protect you naturally after that.

If you ask right away, and the lone-wolf is a man and you're a woman or a young man (or otherwise deemed by them as "naturally weaker") it is possible that they will feel some natural instinct to protect you. Just because they appear to lack the "Robin Hood" attitude of a Guardian Dog, does not mean that they don't have it latent within them to some degree. If they agree to help you, for whatever reason, congratulations! Keep up your relationship, express gratitude and try to find out if you can help them with anything. Being of a sensitive or "weaker" nature, it's likely that you have the ability to find out, even from a lone-wolf, if they need help with anything (which you of course do— within reason). Also try to learn from them whatever you can learn in terms of inner strength.

If you ask but they reject you, it is possible that they view you as "a man in your best years" (or otherwise deemed by them as "naturally strong"). They may feel that you should be able to stand up for yourself. Because lone-wolves are strong and fearless and independent by nature, they can have a hard time realizing that everyone is not the same and can simply be of the opinion that you are a coward who, if you just pull yourself together, can act like they do. So, it's not necessarily that they don't care—they may just find it hard to understand your fear/weakness. In this case you can try to explain to them that everyone is not naturally as strong as they are, and hope they will help you.

If you prefer to slowly build up a relationship in the hopes that they will protect you naturally after that, keep in mind that lone-wolves by nature usually don't strive to have "friends"—but the concept of a mutual exchange of ideas and favors is usually alright with them, and is often the closest you'll get to becoming "friends" with them. Just the fact that they accept you is a step in the right direction. Again, being of a sensitive or "weaker" nature, it's likely that you have the ability to find out, even from a lone-wolf, if they need help with anything, work-related or otherwise—perhaps a mutual interest or even a hobby. If you manage to cement this relationship, they are much more likely to tell the bully off should they attack you, because then they are attacking someone who helps them!

If it does not work out with one lone-wolf, try the next one on your list. If you can't get any lone-wolf to help you to your satisfaction, go to Option 3.

Option 3: Dealing With The Bully With The Help Of Bullied Co-Workers

If you are the softer, non-confrontational personality and for various reasons won't or can't deal with the bully yourself, and feel that your workplace/country has non-existent or non-functional behavior codex/laws, and/or that your boss/trade union is not able or willing to support you, and you can't find a strong ally or they are not willing or able to help you, or if you don't want to be seen as "weak" by asking your boss/trade union for help or take legal measures, then your best option is to deal with the bully with support and comfort from "fellow sufferers"—other bullied co-workers.

It's usually quite obvious to a bullied person who the bullied ones are. It's simply the other ones who are being laughed and pecked at. But if the workplace is big there may be more bullies in other departments, and with some observation you will probably be able to spot others in the same situation, if there are any.

When you have listed them, approach them one by one discretely and talk about it. Form a "Bullied People's Association" and arrange secret meetings if you feel it's the right thing to do. Pinpoint how many bullies there are, analyze how each and every one of you have dealt with them so far, and compare your methods and the results.

Being in a group of fellow sufferers is better than being totally alone. You can find comfort in each other and in the fact that your fellow sufferer(s) understand you totally, and that you are actually better off than the laughing sheep that have reached an end station and will in all likelihood stay there, with the bully as their "boss". You may even feel brave enough together to approach and challenge the bully. If so, great!

Keep in mind, however, that every coin has two sides. There is also a danger that by socializing exclusively with each other, you will cement your own belief that you are not strong, and accept this to the degree that being bullied becomes your unquestioned life style. It's a bit like the 1984 high school comedy movie *Revenge of the Nerds* where it's actually fun being a bullied "nerd"—with a fitting nerd laugh and an IQ as high up as their trousers around their waists!

If you notice that this is the case, you need to decide for yourself—or as a group if you have formed one—if you want to stay that way, or if you want to work on becoming strong and being able to stand up for yourself. Remember, it's much easier if you all make the same decision so that you can continue to support each other. If you decide to become strong, see *Chapter 3 - Building Up Your Inner Strength* and *Chapter 6 – Forming an Anti-Bully Group*. Know that it may be a long road to walk, but the rewards are worth it. Just imagine walking up to the bully together, fearlessly—would that not feel better than constantly trying to avoid the bully? Having said that, only you know what suits you best.

Option 4: Dealing With The Bully Yourself Via A Letter

If you prefer to or need to deal with the bully alone and you are a "soft" non-confrontational personality and want to avoid direct involvement with the bully as much as possible, your best option is to write the bully a "smart" letter. Even if a personal confrontation may be more efficient and even appear impressive to the bully, some people will simply not feel strong enough for an eye-to-eye confrontation whatever they do, and this indirect method is much better than not doing anything at all. While I naturally cannot, and should not, tell you word for word what to write, because that will depend on your personal situation, a generic example that you can adapt would be this:

A) "John Smith" (or whatever their full name is). Always write their full name; it will send them subconscious signals that you are not afraid of them. In films, often when someone stands up to someone, they use their full name. Think about it: calling your bully "John Smith" makes them less likeable and human than if you call them "John", does it not?

B) "I don't appreciate it when you [whatever they say or do]." Drag their deeds into the light. Be specific. Avoid generalizations like "treat me like garbage" or exaggerations, as that will put the bully on defense—keep to the facts. For example: "When you call me names in front of others".

C) "You are only trying to make me look stupid in front of these people." By pinpointing someone's (more or less) hidden *intentions* and showing them that you are aware of it, they will possibly find it less fun to "play with you". Your letter will also be less fun for them to show around to others.

D) "You stop that now." "Stop" and "now" are both "subconscious power words", meaning they signal "power" to the subconscious mind of anyone reading those words. If you think about it, most people who use these words confidently and efficiently are in a power position.

E) "Or I will [some suitable legal threat]." "Suitable" here means something that you know or strongly suspect will have a deterring effect on the bully—don't try to scare them with some weak boss or by being vague ("Or else..."). Only you know what will have an effect here, but here are some examples that you could adapt to your situation: "report you to [an executive you know they have respect for]", or "be wearing a recorder at all times and record you" or "file a lawsuit on you for [harassment, etc.]." If you're not certain, go for the biggest (lawsuit). If you can't find any suitable thing to threaten them with, see *Chapter 7 – Dirty Tricks & Bluffs: Should You Use Them?* You must also make sure that the threat is legal. To write "I'd watch my back if I were you" (or something similar), could be interpreted as an implied illegal threat in many countries. Even if it's unlikely that the bully would file a lawsuit against you (because that would probably make him look scared of you in front of his ever-present admirers!) it is still illegal.

If they are only bullying you, sign the letter with your name if you feel you want to or feel it's needed. If they are bullying others as well, sign the letter with your name if you feel you want to or you feel it's needed, or alternatively sign it "one of the people you bully"—that will possibly scare them, as now they can't know who will file a lawsuit or who will be wearing a recorder (even should it be illegal!).

Option 5: Dealing With The Bully Yourself Eye-To-Eye

You can confront the bully eye-to-eye in two different ways, depending on how "tough" you feel. If you prefer confronting the bully in a "softer" way when they are alone, choose Alternative 1. It can also be a good idea to start with Alternative 1 and thus give your bully a chance to "surrender" without having to "defend their honor" in front of their admirers. If you prefer a more confrontational way in front of their "admirers"—perhaps because you have worked up your confidence enough using the preparatory steps, or if you tried Alternative 1 and it did not work—then choose Alternative 2.

Confronting the Bully - Alternative 1: The "Soft" Way

As long as the bullies have their "admirers" around them (usually most of the time!) they will also have their "guard up" because they will feel a need to demonstrate to them who the leader is. If you were to approach the bully when everyone were looking, and ask the bully to stop, they would only escalate their attack on you. Even if you asked kindly, the bully would probably not stop, even if they wanted to, because if they did as you asked it would be like telling their admirers, "I am weak. May I present to you our new leader".

If you, on the other hand, pick a moment when the bully is alone, they will have their "guard down" because they would feel no immediate need to "defend their status". Pick a time when you believe the bully will be alone for at least five minutes—being interrupted after a minute will totally change the bully's attitude towards you and ruin your chances. If you study them, perhaps you will discover some predictable moments in their daily schedule when they are usually alone.

Assuming you have already done the preparatory steps in Chapter 3, approach the bully in a neutral way—not too fast and not too slow. Position yourself about 3-4 feet (ca 1 meter) from them. If you stand too close you will invade their personal space and it would look like you're attacking them, and if you stand too far away you will appear afraid and they will take no notice of you. (If the idea of standing this close to the bully makes you feel uncomfortable, I suggest you go back and review the preparatory steps in chapter 3, and possibly use NLP or EFT.)

Keep your arms relaxed by your sides. If you cross your arms or keep your hands resting on your hips like a Hollywood cowboy or behind you like a policeman the bully will see you as confrontational and up their guard, and if you keep your hands clasped in front of you like a preacher they will see you as weak and pleading. Keep your head straight; don't lean it sideways or keep your chin up—that would look like you have an "attitude" and they would think you're challenging them. Look the bully straight in the eyes. But don't look overly aggressive as that may, once again, trigger their "guard up" (yes, bullies are very sensitive in this aspect). Remember that inner strength also comes from acting in a way that feels natural to you, or it will feel and look fake. So, if needed, practice standing like this until it feels natural.

What you say now, and how you say it, is of utmost importance and crucial to increasing your chances of them listening to you. There is a "formula" which, when used properly, ensures that you really get your point across without offending the other person unnecessarily. The formula was developed by Marshall B. Rosenberg and is called NVC—Nonviolent Communication. In short, NVC has four steps: A) Observe the facts. B) Tell how you feel. C) Tell what your needs are. D) Tell what you request. While I naturally cannot, and should not, tell you word for word what to say, because that depends on your personal situation, a generic example that you can adapt would be this:

Step A: "John, you have been calling me names in front of others at least every week since I started here." Don't ask

"May I have a word with you?" before you start. If you ask for permission to talk then you're giving them a chance to reject you before you have even begun. Also, avoid generalizations and exaggerations as that will put the bully on defense—keep to the facts ("at least every week since I started here").

Step B: "This makes me angry and frustrated." Avoid "sad" as that *may* be just what they want to hear. By staying relatively unemotional and using "strong" negative emotions (as opposed to "weak" negative emotions) you avoid appearing unnecessarily vulnerable.

Step C: "Because I need to feel respected, just like everybody else here." Not an unreasonable request, is it?

Step D: "So I kindly ask you not to do that." In this case I suggest you avoid "ask you to *stop*" since "stop" is a "power word" that the bully will (subconsciously) associate with powerful people and thus feel you are ordering them, which could backfire on you.

Steps A through D should be spoken fluently, with no obvious pause in between; I am only dividing them here to make the individual steps more obvious. Make sure you have practiced beforehand what to say. If you hesitate, you will not appear confident and the bully will sense that right away. If needed, practice at home until you can say it fluently and fearlessly.

After you have said what you wanted to say, stop talking and keep your eye contact with the bully. Say and do nothing until you get a reaction from them. If they react with *anger* and rudely ask you to go away, start a negotiation by calmly asking them, "What would it take for you to stop? " (At this point you have little to lose by using the word "stop" because it's part of a question, not a request.) If they insist in their anger, just leave and go on to Alternative 2. If they start to talk, listen carefully to what they have to say, as you have now possibly opened up a dialogue. Chances are they will be honest and tell you why they act like they do, and if so, this *may* be your first step to solving the situation! If their reply is not honest (sarcastic, etc.) just leave and go on to Alternative 2.

If they *deny* it all, don't try to make them confess. That would be futile—what could they possibly gain from confessing? The good thing is, if they deny it, it means you got them where it hurts, because obviously they know what they did; but at the same time, since they *deny* it, it also means that they know what they did was *wrong*—a weak spot that you will now use to your advantage. Since public denial (as opposed to internal self-denial) is based on fear of being "caught", say "If you ever do that again I will record you and send the proof to everyone" (whether you intend to or not!). The generalization "everyone" is great here for causing stress! Then immediately turn around and walk away. Don't ask questions like, "Are we clear?" Just leave them wondering. If they shout "I fear no one" or "Don't you dare" or "Come back here", that's a good sign that your method has worked, because the bully would not act strongly emotionally if they didn't feel compromised. The proof of the pudding, however, is in the eating. Notice if they change their behavior or not. If they continue, go to Alternative 2. If not, congratulations! You outsmarted the bully, who will probably pick an easier target from now on.

If they simply say "no", then don't just accept that and walk away. Instead, quickly ask, "Why?" If they start to explain why, listen carefully to what they have to say. Chances are they will tell you why they act like they do, and if so, this *may* be your first step to solving the situation! If their reply is "because" (or sarcastic, etc.), start a negotiation by asking them "*What would it take for you to stop?*" If they start to talk, listen carefully to what they have to say. If their reply is honest and they seem to be "open for negotiation" this *may* be your first step to solving the situation! If their reply is not honest (or sarcastic, etc.) just leave and go on to Alternative 2.

Confronting the Bully - Alternative 2: The "Tough" Way

If the previous "soft" alternative did not work for you, or if you have worked up your confidence enough using the preparatory steps to "grab the bully by the horns" and confront them right then and there in an in-face style in front of their "admirers", then this is your best option.

Assuming you have already done any needed preparatory steps in Chapter 3, let's start with some "don'ts" when it comes to your first step. Do *not* put up an unnecessarily aggressive "fight" or call them names, etc.—that will look like you are challenging them in front of their group and will escalate the confrontation. Remember, this is a workplace, not your private battle ground, and there are company rules to follow. Do *not* plead or beg them to "be kind", etc.—pleading is for "Alternative 1: The Soft Way" and would only make it worse if the bully's "admirers" are watching, and that would increase the bully's apparent power over you. Do *not* walk away "with your tail between your legs", appearing defeated or humiliated—once again these reactions are just what the bully wants and will only encourage them to continue!

The first thing you *should* do when the bully attacks you is to consciously choose the emotion that will work best for you here, namely anger—or more specifically "focused anger", not "explosively" angry like Donald Duck. Remember what you read in the part "How your subconscious views whom the bully is attacking" in the NLP section of chapter 3. Bring to mind someone you love dearly and feel very protective about, and then imagine that the bully is attacking not only you, but also the person you love (who is standing next to you). This will most likely bring out "blind anger" in you, meaning anger unaffected by any sort of fear. This shift of emotion will take place instantly because "fear" hormones and "anger" hormones are basically identical. Practice "feeling angry" privately, using the visualization above, until you can be angry at will. It's like acting, but your body and mind will believe that you really are angry, and will work with you.

In order to back up your inner emotion of anger, you need an equally strong external body language: Stand upright— try to be as tall as possible. At the same time keep your head slightly lowered by leaning your chin slightly downwards. This has two advantages: It will give you a more "menacing" look than if you keep your chin up in an overtly aggressive way or if you merely kept it straight and neutral. It will also appear as if you are looking down on them, both psychologically and physically. (If the bully is taller than you are, you only need to keep your eyes aimed higher.) Keep your arms by your sides, slightly tensed with your hands forming a fist; but not too tight—it should only be sending subtle signals to the bully's subconscious, which registers everything. Remember to act in a way that feels natural to you, or it will feel and look fake; so practice standing like this at home in front of the mirror until it feels so natural that you could fool even yourself.

You also need an equally strong facial expression. Look the bully straight in the eyes, with an angry but not overly aggressive look. The secret to "dangerously angry eyes" lies in the black/white ratio: the more your (dark) pupils show in comparison to the white of your eyes, the more dangerous you will look. To get the right kind of look in your eyes, experiment in front of a mirror by contracting the small muscles that control your lower as well as upper eyelids, in combination with the muscles that control your eyebrows, until you have found an expression that makes you look angry in a menacing and totally fearless way. (Again, the purpose of this is mainly to send subtle signals to the bully's subconscious, even though it will also have some effects on a conscious level.)

Now, practice combining your inner feeling of anger, your body language and your facial expression in front of a mirror until you can do it automatically and instantly. If you can do it with eyes closed, and when you open them menacingly it's just right, ten times in a row, you've got it! This "power combination" will "break the bully's pattern" by introducing something that throws them off in their usually very "in-control" world; and it will give you a few undisturbed moments to deliver your message—which is all you need.

Now the time has come to speak up in a way that backs up your tough and fearless body language. If you say something wrong or "weak" now, you could easily ruin everything. Consistency is the key here. While I naturally cannot, and should not, tell you word for word what to say, because that will depend on your personal situation, a generic example that you can adapt would be this:

Step A: "John Smith" (or whatever their full name is). Always say their full name. It will place everyone's attention on them instead of on you, and at the same time it will send them subconscious signals that you are not afraid of them. In films, often when someone stands up to someone, they use their full name. Think about it: calling your bully "John Smith" makes them less likeable and human than if you call them "John", does it not?

Step B: "I don't appreciate it when you [whatever they say or do]." Drag their deeds into the light. Be specific. Avoid generalizations like "treat me like garbage" or exaggerations, as that will put the bully on defense—keep to the facts. For example: "When you call me names in front of others". Also avoid blaming them unnecessarily, as that will increase the risk of them interrupting you. Remember, talking is their strength, so don't let them drag you into a word-fight. The key here is to deliver your message quickly, in one continuous flow.

Step C) "You are only trying to make me look stupid in front of these people." By pinpointing someone's (more or less) hidden *intentions* and dragging it out into the light, that person tends to lose their power, because part of the power lies in the fact that their underlying intention was not outspoken, but implied. It's a bit like explaining a joke in detail—it's simply not as funny anymore.

Step D) "You stop that now." "Stop" and "now" are both "subconscious power words", meaning they signal "power" to the subconscious mind of anyone hearing those words. If you think about it, most people who use these words confidently and efficiently are in a power position.

Step E) "Or I will [some suitable legal threat]." "Suitable" here means something that you know or strongly suspect will have a deterring effect on the bully—don't try to scare them with some weak boss or by simply saying "or else..." (If you say "or else..." then they are likely to cockily respond with "or what?" and if you have not prepared a really good answer, you will most likely be the laughing stock of the week!) Only you know what will have an effect here, but here are some examples that you could adapt to your situation: "report you to [an executive you know they have respect for]", or "be wearing a recorder at all times and record you" or "file a lawsuit against you for [harassment, etc.]." If you're not certain, go for the biggest (lawsuit). If you can't find any suitable thing to threaten them with, see *Chapter 7 – Dirty Tricks & Bluffs: Should You Use Them?*

You must also make sure that the threat is legal. To say, "I'd watch my back if I were you" or "If I were you I would be really careful of what I say" could be interpreted as an implied illegal threat in many countries. Even if it's unlikely that the bully would file a lawsuit against you (because that would probably make him look scared of you in front of his ever-present admirers!) it is still illegal and there would be witnesses as well to testify against you. For the same reason, avoid a common cliche like "Or I will kick your butt". You have probably never stood up to the bully before, so the bully and their admiring audience would hardly believe you would "kick their butt"! And besides, physical violence is illegal in many countries unless you need to protect yourself against a clear and present physical danger.

Now practice alone saying the entire phrase that you have decided upon based on Steps A through E, until you can do so fluently and convincingly ten times in a row. Finally, practice combining your inner feeling of anger, your body language, your facial expression and the phrases (A - E) in front of a mirror until you can do it convincingly ten times in a row. Why ten times? Because in a real situation you will be less relaxed than when practicing alone, so if you only practice for one repetition you are more likely to fail "in the real world". Now, and only now, are you ready to do the actual confronting. Should you still feel too nervous when facing the bully, it's better to go back and review all the steps again and "rehearse" and prepare more, than to make a half-hearted effort. You are ready when you are ready, not before.

After you have delivered your "line", don't wait for a reply, and don't get involved in a discussion! Remember that talking is *their* strength. Instead, just say what you must, turn around immediately and walk away. If they start to object, just leave right in the middle of their sentence—it's not like they can order you to listen. In this way *you* are in control, not them. You got the final word. Have you ever seen a (good) police officer get involved in a negotiation? No. They tell the offender what they did wrong, hand them a ticket, then leave. That is authority. That is power.

There will probably be a silence after this, from everyone. And because "sheep" are psychologically weak they are not necessarily loyal, but may follow the strongest—and right now that is quite possibly you! Some of them will probably be impressed that you stood up to the bully. If the reaction from their "sheep flock" isn't what the bully expected (silence instead of laughter and awe) the bully will probably feel less motivated to bully you again, because they primarily draw their energy and motivation from the reactions of their "admirers".

It's possible that the bully will try a second time to "save their honor" when they have collected themselves. If they do, you will have prepared a short "statement" such as, "Did I not tell you to stop? Give me *one* good reason not to [whatever you threatened them with!]" If they seem to back off, it may be tempting for you to say "Good. Next time I will, I promise you!" but it may be smarter at this point to just remain silent. If they are still trying to bully you, tell them, "Okay, I tried to warn you, you brought this upon yourself", and then walk away, leaving them wondering whether you will do whatever you threatened to do (which is of course up to you, but they will never know for sure).

By now they should have realized that you are not a sheep, but another wolf, a lone-wolf who stands up for yourself, and they will leave you alone. They will also probably dislike you intensely. But remember that being "liked" by a bully is only possible if you are their sheep—a bully typically either "likes" (in their own distorted way) or dislikes, there is usually no in between.

It is quite possible that you have inspired some of their "followers" and that they will approach you, discretely, to express their admiration. It may even have dawned on them that deep inside they actually dislike the bully but are afraid to oppose him and instead they have chosen the easy way: to be part of the sheep flock and laugh at the bully's victims.

Option 6: Dealing With The Bully Yourself - The "Don't Mess With Me" Way

This last option is for you who were "born tough" and prefer to "grab the bully by the horns" and show them who they are dealing with right then and there in front of everyone (or possibly if you have worked your confidence up to this level by now!) In all likelihood you are prone to anger, and being confrontational has been a natural thing to you throughout life. If so, you're actually at an advantage because you were born tough, whereas most bullies are cowards deep inside. Therefore "winning the fight" is not an issue here—you will most likely do that anyway—but your main concern here is winning *without causing a fight*, at least not if you can avoid it, because it would disturb others. Remember that this is a workplace situation, not a private situation.

While it may be tempting and even natural for you to start calling them names or "put them down" in various ways, remember that because you are a strong personality you are probably seen as a potential threat by the bully. If you start calling them names, they could interpret that as a direct attempt from you to take over their position as a "social leader", which could escalate the situation totally out of proportion.

Instead, you need to confront the bully in a "smart" way that: A) shows that you are *not* interested in "taking over" their position as social leader; B) makes it absolutely clear to them that you want them to leave you alone; C) shows them that you are not the slightest bit afraid of them. This involves both your body language, what you say and how you say it. Here are some examples: "You-leave-me-alone!" or "You-back-off!" or "You-stay-off-my-back, unless-it-is-absolutely-necessary-for-the-job!" (The hyphens between each word means that you should make a micro pause in between each word.) Make it as brief as possible. Stand relatively close to them and point your index finger directly at them while looking straight into their eyes. Being a born confrontational personality, this is probably something you do very well without needing instructions or practicing!

That should do the trick. If it doesn't, you need to ask yourself if you're the tough person you thought you were, or if you indeed felt some degree of fear. If so, you may want to reconsider if this is the right option for you—there are five more to choose from. In any case there should be enough information in this book to help you, just keep reading.

Chapter 6 – Forming an Anti-Bully Group (Optional)

Remember the famous three little monkeys? One covering its own eyes with its hands, the second covering its own ears and the third its own mouth? That is a symbol for the old proverb that "The only thing necessary for the triumph of evil is for good men to do nothing"—see no evil, hear no evil, speak no evil.

After you have successfully dealt with the bully, either alone or with the help of others, you can either choose to stop there and relax and go about your life; or you could go a step further and prevent the bully from further bullying, by forming an "anti-bully group" with other strong, like-minded people. What will make your group strong is the fact that every single member supports each other, making you strong as a group. The "bad" group, lead by the bully, consists of just one strong (but cowardly) person (the bully), and possibly a couple of semi-strong sub-leaders—the rest are just weak and will-less sheep who will blindly follow the strongest person (often regardless of whether that person is good or bad).

So, who should you approach and ask to join the group? Bullied co-workers (see *Chapter 5 Option 3*) and strong allies ("lone-wolves") (see *Chapter 5 Option 2*). If you haven't done so already, read those chapters, do some observation, and write down any person who is suitable for your group.

Start with other bullied persons, as they are probably most likely to want to join. Approach them when no one is around, and simply present your idea. As your group grows, tell the person you approach about the people who have joined already (alternatively, bring every member with you).

Next, approach the lone-wolves. You need them for their strength and fearlessness. They may or may not want to be in a group, but chances are they feel lonely at work, even if they are a lone-wolf. Don't overwhelm them with, "Oh, we're gonna have so much fun together and meet and…" Remember, they are lone-wolves—so take it easy and simply ask them "to be part of an anti-bully network" with no strings attached. That will give them the contact possibilities that they possibly need, without obligations to meet and "socialize". Don't push them to make up their mind then and there; if they hesitate, ask them to think about it and let them know you will check again in a week or so. Lone-wolves usually hate feeling pressured, and a week to think it over will help them feel at ease.

Don't bother approaching the bully's "followers" to convince them to be on your side. You only want independent people in your group who will not "change sides" at any moment. Let them approach you instead, if they are interested. In this way they will have made the decision on their own, which is a sign of inner strength. In this way you will keep your group homogenous—every single member is strong and independent (just make sure that every member also has high ethical standards).

Next, select three of you to be the group's "enforcement ambassadors". Only one will have no "group" effect, two *could* be enough if your group is small, but three is best. Four or more would make it look like a riot and should be avoided. Select the psychologically toughest and/or most articulate one of you as "spokesman", and the two biggest ones as the spokesman's strong and silent "body guards" .

When confronting the bully, do so when they are alone. This is to avoid a "wild west" situation. The spokesman should position himself relatively close in front of the bully, point their index finger (or alternatively their entire hand in "military style") directly at them, look straight into their eyes, and with a menacing voice and facial expression say,

"You-leave-our-friend-alone!" Or, the longer version: "You-stay-off-our-friend, unless-it-is-absolutely-necessary-for-the-job!" (The hyphens between each word means that you should make a micro pause in between each word.) Always mention "friend" so that the bully does understand that they are attacking a friend of yours. The two "body guards" will stand on each side of the spokesman, slightly behind him, remaining silent, with their feet relatively wide apart and arms crossed over their chests, with a stern (but not directly threatening) look on their faces and their eyes focused on the bully. (I suggest you all practice in front of a mirror first.)

Performed right this will intimidate the bully, both psychologically and physically, as they are probably not used to being confronted by three tough people at once. And rather than risking being confronted by all three of you in front of their admirers, and thus being seen as weak, they will leave that particular person alone.

And voila! Now, instead of being bullied, you are the bully police. And who knows, maybe you will enjoy this new power so much that you just can't wait for the bully to find a new victim—if they dare that is, because the bully will sooner or later figure out that every person they bully just so happens to be your friend.....

Chapter 7 – Dirty Tricks & Bluffs: Should You Use Them?

Revenge is a natural thing to some people when they feel unfairly treated, and it may be tempting to pull off a "dirty trick" in order to humiliate the bully in front of everyone, like having a florist deliver a "singing love telegram" from another man, if the bully is a straight man (this is an actual example taken from the generally non-available, *The Avenger's Handbook*). But you need to think two or three steps ahead here. Just because you *could* humiliate the bully, doesn't mean you *should*. And the reason for that is because you never know what reaction you might trigger in them if you ridicule them publicly. (Besides, remember that this is a workplace, not your private battle ground, and there are rules to follow.)

As you know by now, bullies are extremely sensitive about how they are viewed by their admirers. So ridiculing them could, from a psychological point of view, be equal to robbing a regular person of their family, their honor, social value, house, money and friends—in short, everything. You don't know the bully's psychological profile or what you may trigger. There is no guarantee that they will not react by shooting people in uncontrolled anger, and you don't want that on your conscience, do you? Also, remember that there is a point where the bullied can become the bully. Don't stoop to that level yourself.

A method in the moral and legal "gray zone" is threatening to reveal embarrassing, shameful or otherwise compromising details about someone's private life (things that you have found either by asking people or through internet researching or through a private detective). Only you can decide if this is the right thing for you. But if you choose this method, make sure that: A) it's your last resort apart from resigning from your job; B) it is legal (check your local laws); C) your purpose is only to use it as psychological leverage to stop the bully from harassing you and (hopefully) never having to reveal it.

Keep in mind that there is a big difference between using dirty tricks to humiliate the bully, and using bluffs to get the psychological leverage you need in order to make the bully stop. As you may remember, in Options 4 & 5 in Chapter 5 (Dealing with the bully yourself via a letter & Dealing with the bully yourself eye-to-eye the "tough" way), Step E included giving the bully a "suitable legal threat". That does not exclude a "false" threat—a bluff. If you can't find a "true" threat that is efficient enough to stop the bully, then you could, at least theoretically, make one up as long as it's still a legal threat. If so, make sure it's likely that the bully will believe you and it's something that they can't verify (never involve another person against their consent, e.g. claiming that your boss has reported them).

For example, if it's not legal where you live to record someone without their knowledge and use it as evidence in court, the bully is probably not aware of that (awareness of laws and rules typically isn't a bully's strength) and they will probably believe you will carry a hidden recorder with you from now on if you threaten them with that. It's not likely the bully—Mr. King of The Workplace—will report you and thus show everyone that they are afraid of you, is it? And even if you *would* carry a small recorder, it's probably not illegal to wear it, only to use it. And even if you will not wear one, how could they be certain you won't?

Other ways to bluff "suitable legal threats" are to send an anonymous note or email to the bully stating: "Leave that poor guy alone. I am sick and tired of you bullying him, and will report you to [boss/authorities] if you don't stop today" and then let the bully worry about *who* is on your side! Or, you could try: "I have evidence" (in connection with some "legal threat" you use) or that you will file a lawsuit against them, even if you don't intend to. (You could even send them copies of the filled out papers—the bully doesn't know whether you actually intend to hand them over to the authorities or not.) Only you know what will work in your unique situation—as always, use your judgment.

Epilogue

As a final word of advice, remember that the bully does not have any actual power over you—they only have the power that you *allow* them to have. And the way that you *allow* people to treat you, is the way that you are *training* them to treat you.

About Jonas Warstad

Born in 1965 in Sweden, and still a Swedish citizen, I have always been interested in the unknown. The unfathomable. The mysteries of the mind. "Secret Knowledge". And for as long as I remember I have also been an avid reader of books on popular psychology, popular science, body language, positive thinking, philosophy, meditation, unexplained mysteries, the power of the mind and various healing modalities—anything that expanded my inner world, and explained the outer world.

As a free thinker I was never really interested in any "formal" psychology training; I was more into strategic thinking, psychological tactical skills, "secret mental tricks"—all in order to find the "magic phrase" or "magic way" to deal with all sorts of people. I believe my interest in dealing with people has a lot to do with the fact that I recognize myself in the typical traits for HSP—Highly Sensitive Person; I always prefer for everyone to be happy, and treat each other respectfully. Through harsh "reality checks" I have also come to realize that I suffer from what is commonly known as "face blindness" (Prosopagnosia). This means that I have the questionable "ability" to talk with someone, and afterward I would typically be unable to describe or draw their face using any details at all other than "well, she had lips, eyes, long hair, a nose, and two ears". For these reasons, my main lasting impression of people is, and has always been, "emotional impressions", such as their mood, and their likes and dislikes (I can often recall if a person likes "pear flavor" or a specific movie or song years after the fact). Interestingly, several relatives of mine, both on my father's and my mother's side, are also more or less "psychic" in various ways. I myself have never had the ability to "see" things (I wish I could see the winning Lottery numbers though!), but my general sensitivity is keen, for good and for bad.

In recent years, around 2010, I started to study a new range of "self-improvement" methods and techniques. I bought books and distance courses as well as "real" courses in body language, micro facial expressions, NLP (Neuro-Linguistic Programming), life coaching, EFT (Emotional Freedom Techniques), Law of Attraction, hypnosis, energy medicine, etc., as well as various self defense techniques. All of these techniques were like "Version 2.0" of everything I had read previously, and gave me a lot of power in life.

Nowadays I'm also a part time instructor in many of these techniques. While this may sound like I "try to know everything", it is in fact no more than my never-ending curiosity about how to improve one's life. Having a broad knowledge puts things in a bigger perspective, and helps me realize how everything is connected. In the end it is also about the concept of peace and power—without both, you have neither.

Connect with Jonas Warstad

www.jonaswarstad.com

www.facebook.com/JonasWarstadAuthor

www.discog.info (one of the largest music discography sites in the world)

Other Books by Jonas Warstad

The Psychopath Exposed: Understanding and Dealing with an Emotional Predator

The Secrets of Dealing with Difficult and Annoying Co-Workers

The Art of Smart: How to Be a Social Genius in the Workplace

Why Criticism Hurts: A Quick Guide on How to Give Criticism in a Loving Way

Yello: Stella — The Story Behind the Album

P.S. One Last Thing...

If you found this book useful we would be very grateful if you'd post a short review on Amazon. Your support really does make a difference and will help others gain the same knowledge that you now have. If you have any ideas or suggestions that you feel would make this book even better, please contact the author through his site www.jonaswarstad.com. He will read your email personally.

Thanks again for your support!

Printed in Great Britain
by Amazon